The Divorce Resource Series

Finding Your Place

A Teen Guide to Life in a Blended Family

Julie Leibowitz

THE ROSEN PUBLISHING GROUP, INC. NEW YORK

To Mom and Al, my blended family

Published in 2000 by The Rosen Publishing Group, Inc.
29 East 21st Street, New York, NY 10010

Copyright © 2000 by The Rosen Publishing Group, Inc.

First Edition

Library of Congress Cataloging-in-Publication Data

Leibowitz, Julie.
    Finding your place: a teen guide to life in a blended family/ Julie Leibowitz.
        p. cm.— (The divorce resource series)
    Includes bibliographical references and index.
    Summary: Explains the complex emotions and relationships involved in the
  remarriage of a parent and examines relationships with stepparents and stepsiblings.
    ISBN 0-8239-3114-5
    1. Stepfamilies— Juvenile literature. 2. Remarriage— Juvenile literature.
  3. Stepchildren— Family relationships— Juvenile literature. 4. parent and teenager—
  Juvenile literature.   [1. Stepfamilies. 2. Remarriage.] I. Title. II. Series.
  HQ759.92.L43 1999
  306.874—dc21   99-048527

Manufactured in the United States of America

Contents

Introduction

Janet's parents were divorced. Every weekend she and her sister, Emily, went to stay with their father and stepmother, Sarah, and Sarah's kids, Danny and Joy. Janet's father and stepmother had also just had a baby girl, Nina. She was Janet's half sister. Janet did not like Nina that much, though. She was always crying, and Janet's father and Sarah never seemed to do anything else except feed her and change her. Janet never really felt comfortable there. There were so many people running around, and it was always so chaotic that Janet did not feel as though she fit in anywhere. It always seemed as if Sarah's kids and the baby were paid a lot of attention, whereas Janet and Emily just kind of blended into the background.

New siblings can cause
feelings of jealousy.

During the week, Janet and Emily lived with their mother and stepfather. Their stepfather, Nick, had a son named Peter from a previous marriage. Peter's mother had died in a car accident when Peter was two years old. Peter and Janet were the same age, but Peter did not like any of the same things as Janet. He did not play sports or video games; he was quiet and read books most of the time. Janet did not really have anything to talk about with Peter, or with her mother and stepfather.

Janet and Emily spent Christmas Eve with their dad and Christmas Day with their mom. They went to their dad's for Thanksgiving every other year, and they went on a trip with him for two weeks at the end of each summer. Janet always had to miss her best friend Doug's birthday party because of the trip. She also missed a lot of softball games on the weekends because her dad was busy doing other things and could not drive her. Janet was upset that she kept missing games, and she was getting really tired of going back and forth between her mom's place and her dad's. Having two blended families was not easy.

According to the Stepfamily Association of America, 65 percent of second marriages involve children from previous marriages. This means that numerous blended families have formed, and perhaps you are a member of one of them, or even two of them if both your natural parents have remarried. Blended families are made up of stepsiblings, blood siblings, and various sets of parents. You personally may have your blood siblings, your stepsiblings, and your stepparents to deal with, or you may be an only child and have just stepparents.

Either way, learning to be part of a blended family is often a difficult challenge, just as the previous scenario describes. Janet is just one example of the many teens who must learn to cope with the complexities of blended-family life, and as a teenager, it is especially difficult to adjust to that life. You are going through so many changes already, and you starting to separate yourself from your parents and family and seek your own identity. These changes are complicated by having to adapt to the dynamics of a new family. You wonder where you fit in.

This book will talk about stepparents and step-siblings and the roles they play in your life. It will discuss the feelings you might be experiencing regarding your new family. You may be very angry or sad, and it is okay to feel that way. If your natural parents are divorced or you have experienced the death of a parent, you will certainly have all kinds of emotions and concerns about new parents and about new families.

Most important, though, this book will explain how to cope best with a blended-family situation, whom you can talk to about your worries and fears, and how to deal with your feelings. You will learn that blended families can be just as wonderful as natural families. In today's society, blended families are not unusual. Like any task, living in a blended family takes work. However, if you make the effort and the other family members do as well, your blended family can be a positive part of your life.

CHAPTER 1

When a Parent Remarries

A blended family is formed when a parent remarries, either after a divorce or the death of a spouse. The parent's new spouse will be a stepparent.

When you find out that one of your parents is getting remarried, you may have many different emotions. You will probably be upset that your parent is going into a marriage with someone else. You may be angry and think that this new person is trying to take the place of your absent parent. Perhaps you are an only child who is living alone with a single parent, and you fear that your stepparent will ruin that special relationship you have with your natural parent. In any case, it is very difficult for a teenager to watch a parent enter into a marriage with someone new.

After Divorce

Seventy-five percent of divorced people remarry, making it fairly likely that if your parents are divorced, one or both of them will get married again. If this happens, you must adjust to having a stepparent and perhaps stepsiblings, who are the children of your parent's new spouse. If you are living with the new family, your daily life will certainly change. You may have to share a room with a stepsibling. You may resent your stepparent for living in the same house as you, a constant reminder that your natural parents live in separate places. Will you still be able to spend time alone with your natural parent? Who will make the rules? Many questions will arise during the formation of the new family.

If your parents are divorced, you are probably still hoping that they will get back together someday. This is a rare event, however, and many kids have difficulty when a parent announces remarriage, mainly because it is a sign that the relationship between the parents is truly over. Trying to accept the situation and move on is the best way to handle it. It is definitely not easy, though, and no one expects you to warm up to the situation right away. But if you think of it in the sense that your life will be better without the tension of your parents' anger toward one another, and that your parents will certainly be happier—and nicer to be around—if they are not living together, you may find that divorce was the best thing.

Entry into a blended family as a teenager is significant in several ways. First, because you are at an age where you are mature enough to be aware of your surroundings and the changes within them, you understand exactly what is happening when your parent remarries. This is good because your parent is made to treat you as an adult and give you all the facts. You are too old for him or her to ignore you or "pull one over on you," as may be the case with much younger children. Also, you are at an age where you are intellectually able to reason and rationalize the situation. Although this is true, that does not necessarily mean that it is easy to listen to the voice of reason and accept your parent's remarriage. That takes a lot of courage, a lot of work, and a lot of time. As a result, this difficult time may be the most important period of growth that you will experienced in your life.

After the Death of a Parent

When a parent has died, it is also difficult to cope with the remarriage of the living parent. You have had to deal with the loss of someone very close to you, and then you must acclimate to living with the person who is filling that role in your life. This is typically a very troubling situation for teens, as they experience a wide variety of emotions. Perhaps they are angry at the living parent for remarrying, and maybe they think that the living parent is trying to "replace" the parent who has died.

It is not that it is more difficult to cope with a blended family if you have

The death of a parent is extremely hard to deal with.

experienced the death of a parent as opposed to divorce; it is simply a different set of factors. Unfortunately the parent who has died is never coming back, whereas in the case of divorce, both of the parents are still alive. The finality of death may become more obvious when a parent remarries and may make it harder to accept the person your parent is marrying. On the other hand, maybe you like your new stepparent but feel that by doing so you are betraying the memory of the parent who died. You need to know that it is possible to like your stepparent and still lovingly remember your parent who has passed away. There is room for both.

You Are Not Alone

If you are in the position of trying to accept your parent's remarriage and you are confused and overwhelmed, know that you are not alone. Second marriages and stepfamilies are so common in today's society that many other teens are in the same situation. You can work your way through it with the help of your family or those outside the family, such as friends or school counselors. The best way to address all types of blended-family situations is through communication. Family roundtable discussions are a good way to get to know the members of the family and to talk about each person's feelings and needs. We will discuss more about family communication in chapter five. Also, talk directly to your natural parent about the feelings and emotions you are experiencing so that he or she can try to help guide you through your adjustment. Remember, it is an adjustment for your parents, too, which we will cover later in the book.

CHAPTER 2

The Myths of Society

Elizabeth could not believe it. Her father had just told her that he was going to marry Ellen, the woman he had been dating for the past year. Ellen was nice, but Elizabeth did not understand why they had to get married. Now Ellen was going to be around all of the time. Elizabeth would not be able to go over to her father's house and spend time just with him anymore. Now Ellen would be there, and so would her two kids, who were only in first grade and third grade. They were babies. Whenever they were all together, no one paid any attention to Elizabeth because Ellen's kids could not do anything by themselves.

Elizabeth told her friend Caroline that her father was going to marry Ellen. "Oooh," Caroline said, "you're going to have a wicked stepmother! I wonder what she's going to do to you! Are you going to be able to play in the soccer game on Saturday? She might make you stay home and scrub the floor."

Elizabeth had not thought about that, but it was true, just like in a fairy tale. Stepmothers were always mean. Elizabeth was very upset. She would probably never be able to play on the soccer team again.

You probably remember from childhood the fairy tales *Snow White and the Seven Dwarfs* and *Cinderella*. In both stories, the main character had a wicked stepmother: a cold and heartless woman, jealous of her stepdaughter's charm and beauty, who punished her by forcing her to perform incessant household duties and forbidding her to leave the house. The characters in these stories have helped to create negative stereotypes of stepparents in our society, particularly stepmothers.

In *Cinderella* there was a wicked stepmother and evil stepsisters. These characters are what most teenagers think of when they picture being part of a stepfamily, so from the start, teens have a distorted perception of how their stepfamily will work. It is

Accepting a stepparent can be tough.

because of this misconception that you must try harder and harder to do away with these stereotypes.

It is important to understand that the stereotypes from these fairy tales are not universally true. Just because your parent is getting remarried does not mean that your step-parent will take an instant dislike to you and force you to lead a miserable life, nor will your stepsiblings taunt you and make you their slave. The fact that you are an important person in your parent's life will make you an important person in your step-parent's life, and because of that, he or she will want to develop a good relation-ship with you.

Remember, *Cinderella* is just a fairy tale.

Stepsiblings

The same misconceptions about stepparents are often associated with stepsiblings, too. In the beginning, although things may not be quite as easy as television shows such as *The Brady Bunch* portray, odds are you will not be in a *Cinderella* situation either. Adolescence is one of the most difficult times in life to have to start living with brand-new people, particularly if other teens are involved. Everyone's emotions are heightened, and as a teenager, the last thing you want is to deal with somebody else's changes, confusion, or mood swings. You have enough to handle in your own life.

Just as your stepparent is going to play an important role in your life, so are your stepsiblings. After all, your parents have gotten married, and now you are all part of the same family. As we mentioned earlier, you may end up sharing a room with a stepsibling, putting you in very close quarters. In any case, try to consider your stepsiblings as positive factors in your new blended family. A stepsibling is a kid just like you, trying to fit into a new family.

In fact, a stepsibling can simply be a friend. If you are close in age, this is even more likely to happen. You might be surprised to find that it is nice to have a

stepsibling around, a peer you can talk to—either in addition to your natural siblings or as a sibling you never had.

Half Siblings

At some point in time, your blended family may expand even more if your parent and stepparent decide to have a child together. Since you will have one common natural parent, this child will be your half sibling. For teenagers especially, it is difficult to have a new baby in the house. A baby causes many lifestyle changes for parents and families. As a teenager, it is one more massive change to cope with at a time that is already filled with transformations.

Having a new baby enter the family also stirs up many emotions. You may feel jealous of all the attention the baby gets or annoyed at how helpless he or she is. It is particularly hard to deal with the new baby if you come from divorced parents. The baby may be a strong sign of the existence of your stepfamily and the fact that your natural parents are not together anymore. However, ultimately the baby is your brother or sister, a bond that cannot be broken or ignored. Although from a teenage perspective, it is very hard to identify with a new child, try to understand the baby's

The family on *The Brady Bunch* is a popular example of a blended family.

needs and think of him or her in a more positive way. If your parent and stepparent ask you to help take care of the baby or perform other chores related to the family, be flattered. It means that you are independent and responsible enough to be trusted with your new brother or sister, as well as with other jobs that may make daily life in your household run a little smoother. It is a big step toward adulthood, as we will discuss in the next section.

You and Your Family

As a teenager, you are experiencing many changes. Aside from the standard physical changes of growth, you are also encountering psychological changes. You are slowly becoming an adult, one who is able to make his or her own decisions and who is forming a distinct personality. It is at this point in your life that you begin to separate from your parents and family and become an individual with your own thoughts and beliefs.

These changes are hard enough to deal with on their own, but if you are trying to adjust to a blended family at the same time, they are even more difficult. Just as you are trying to separate from the family and formulate a strong identity, you are simultaneously being pulled into this new group, the blended family, and depended upon to help make it work. If you are in junior high or high school, you have only a few years or so before you go off to college or get a job, move out of your house, and become more independent. These possibilities may make it even harder to focus on being a part of your blended family. It is as though you are growing up and learning to interact with your family all over again while striving toward pursuing personal goals and leading a more autonomous life. It is a challenge, but you can do both. In the next chapter, we will focus on your role in the blended family and how you fit in. You can still be your own person while being a part of your blended family.

CHAPTER 3

How Do You Fit In?

Amy was not very happy. Her father had recently married Kate, who had three sons. Two of them, Steven and Paul, were in high school, and Ben was away at college, so he was not home much. But that did not matter. Steven and Paul were enough by themselves. They were always running around, wrestling with each other, and making a lot of noise when Amy was trying to do her homework.

Amy did not really like guys that much, except for her dad, of course. Ever since her mother died when she was five, Amy had gotten quite used to living with just her dad. Now, though, there were all of these new people in the house. In the evenings after dinner, Amy's dad and Kate played games with the boys and

Stepsiblings—like any siblings—can drive you crazy sometimes!

watched videos, too. Every Thursday someone else got a chance to pick out a movie at the video store for the family to watch. But Amy always skipped her turn. She did not want to watch videos with Kate and the boys. She did not want Kate to be her mother either. Amy just wanted to be alone with her dad the way it used to be. She did not like all of these changes, and she did not feel as though there was really a place for her anyway. Most nights Amy closed the door and stayed alone in her room while the rest of the family were downstairs having fun together.

One of the most difficult challenges to face in considering how you fit into the blended family is the idea of change. Your blended-family life may present some drastic changes from the way your life was before your parent remarried, but it is to your benefit to try to cope with those changes in a positive way. This can be hard, since you may not be all that happy about your parent's remarriage. Also, as a teenager, you are experiencing enough changes already. However, making the best of things can only make your life, and the rest of the family's, more comfortable. Whereas before perhaps you used to walk the dog and take out the garbage, maybe now your responsibilities have changed, so you do the

Your responsibilities may change when your parent remarries.

dishes instead. The parents should be able to decide what responsibilities each child should have so that everyone feels comfortable.

Feeling comfortable, though, is not always so easy. It is a natural part of growing up to feel scared and insecure during adolescence, unsure of who you are and where you fit in. Most teens desperately want to conform to some kind of standard—to be like everyone else, to be cool. Teenagers in blended families often feel excessive pressure. They are trying to make sense of their new family structure and may think of it as another difference that sets them apart, out of the "cool" loop. In addition to the list of normal developmental tasks, teens in blended families have extra challenges to master. Perhaps you have just started middle school, you are trying out for a sports team, and your first school dance is coming up in a few weeks. One of your parents has just gotten remarried, and you suddenly have three stepbrothers. That is a lot to deal with all at once! Take a deep breath and relax.

Adolescence is all about growth and change, and coping with blended families is just one more challenge for teens to face. It might not be easy, but it will undoubtedly make you stronger and enable you to handle just about anything that comes your way.

Fitting in is a big part of teenage life. Most teens yearn to fit in at school, to make a place for themselves in a particular group, and to be popular with their peers. The same ideas apply when considering how a teen fits into his or her blended family. Roles in blended families may not be as clear as in natural families. You may be unsure what your place is and what your responsibilities are. You may not be happy about your parent's remarriage, which makes settling into a blended family even harder. Often your role in the typical family is somewhat structured by birth order: The oldest is the caretaker, and the youngest is the "baby" and is usually the most coddled. Middle children, generally, have a harder time finding their place in the family, as their position in the birth order does not give them a definitive role. In any case, no matter what the birth order of your natural family, your role in the blended family will differ. Maybe you are now the baby-sitter for younger stepsiblings instead of the youngest child, or perhaps you now have siblings when before you were an only child. Your role will carve itself out as time progresses. The responsibilities you had prior to your parent's remarriage may become greater, or they may become even less if there are now more people to share in the duties. You might try to think of this as one of the positives of your blended family.

Feeling Included

Just as most teens worry about fitting in, they also worry about being excluded from a group or activity in a social setting. Once again, this applies to the blended-family situation as well. The way family members relate to each other depends on each person's personality. Perhaps you are quiet and shy, whereas your new stepparent and stepsiblings are more outspoken and aggressive. This may cause you to feel uncomfortable around them and prompt you to withdraw from the group. It is important to realize in a situation like this that no one is excluding you on purpose. You just have different characteristics that may take some getting used to, and the same goes for the rest of the family. Learning to accept other people's differences is something you will certainly have to do in order to help make the blended family work.

Getting yourself involved in family activities is extremely helpful in your adjustment. It is true that if you are indeed shy and have trouble in group situations, this may be hard; however, if you are simply withdrawing because you are angry about your parent's remarriage, you are only making your situation worse. You are letting your resentment and hostility toward the situation prevent you from making the

Togetherness takes
time and patience.

best of things, and you will only find yourself more excluded and isolated. You will also be missing out on what could be a fun, enjoyable family situation. The more involved you are with the family, the more comfortable you will begin to feel in the group and the more you will fit in.

CHAPTER 4

Dealing with Resentment and Anger

Rita's mother was going to marry Jack, whom she had been dating for a few years, and Rita was not very happy about it. Rita had been hoping that her parents would still get back together, and she was very upset that Jack was moving into her house. Was Jack going to eat dinner in the same chair at the dining-room table where Rita's father used to sit? Was he going to come home every night and sit down in the recliner in the den to watch the news, just as Rita's father used to?

Rita did not want Jack sitting at the dining-room table. She wanted her dad back with her and her mom.

As you begin to deal with your new stepparent and his or her role in your life, it is natural to feel some

hostility and resentment. After all, he or she is acting in the role of the parent who no longer lives with you. It is difficult enough to come to terms with the fact that one parent no longer lives in your house, so coping with a new person taking his or her role in the family is not easy. You may also resent the fact that your natural parent now relies upon a new spouse for certain things, whereas before your parent may have relied upon you. It is as though the responsibilities you took on are no longer needed. This is very common in the case of an only child, in which a unique bond exists between the parent and child because it is just the two of them together.

On the other hand, things may become even more confusing if you actually like your stepparent and begin to develop a relationship with him or her. You may feel that you are hurting your absent parent by being friendly with this new person; you feel disloyal. It is similar to the feeling you may have experienced if your parents are divorced, and while spending time with one parent you feel disloyal to the other. However, as time goes on, you will learn that it is okay to like your stepparent; in fact, if you live with your stepparent, it will certainly make everyone's lives much easier if the two of you do get along. After a

It can be difficult to come to terms with a parent's absence.

while, as you continue to grow and mature, you may even realize that by getting along with your stepparent, you have helped to create a new, harmonious family. If your parents are divorced and all you can remember of their marriage is tension and fighting, then the success of your blended family will definitely be a positive influence on your well-being.

What Do You Call Your Stepparent?

An important issue that arises when we talk about feelings toward a stepparent is the name. What are you supposed to call your stepparent? There are a variety of options, and you must do what feels comfortable in your particular situation. Most likely, calling your stepparent "Mom" or "Dad" will not work. Those names symbolize a kinship you established with your natural parents at birth, and they probably will not seem appropriate with anyone else. Once again, though, every stepfamily situation is unique. Perhaps your father has died, and the man your mother is marrying plays an important part in your life. You may want to call him "Dad." It all depends on what the relationship is.

For teenagers, however, being on a first-name basis with their stepparent is the most common scenario. It helps create a casual, warm environment where you can think of your stepparent as your friend. It is important to remember that your stepparent is not a replacement for your parent who no longer lives with you; he or she is simply another parent, an "extra."

Talking About It

Coping with all of these issues and emotions can be trying. Although you are on the path to adulthood, you are not there yet, and attempting to face these issues is a lot to handle all by yourself. You can, of course, talk to your parents. However, many teens find it helpful to talk to someone else, an outsider—someone whom you trust and who can be objective, who can help you wade through the tough issues you are facing, and who can try to make sense out of some of them. There are many people like this who can help you: school psychologists, social workers, and community leaders are just some of them. Talking can really help, particularly if you are dealing with both social issues and family issues. You may be surprised at how a fresh view on things can make the situation a little clearer.

Another outlet that can be a great help in coping is a support group. You may have heard of adult support groups such as Divorced Dads or Parents Without Partners. These are groups that help adults deal with the issues that have affected their lives, such as divorce

or the death of a spouse. There are groups like this for teens as well. You may find one right in your own school, run by a teacher or a school social worker. You may also find them in community centers or at the office of a psychologist. For several reasons, this type of group can be helpful in coming to terms with the issues you are dealing with as a teenager. First, it is often easier to talk about problems in a group setting, where everyone has experienced similar life changes and can identify with your feelings. In a group that focuses on the remarriage of parents and on blended families, you may find it useful to hear other teens' stories and how they are coping. It may give you some ideas on how to adjust to your own situation. The group can also be a good outlet through which to express your anger, sadness, or whatever you are feeling to people who will listen and sympathize. At the end of this book, you will find a section on getting outside help, which lists some of the numerous groups and organizations whose chief concern is giving support to children and parents in blended families.

Parental Jealousies

Sheryl's dad had recently married Paula. Sheryl spent every weekend at their house and actually really

Talking with a counselor or other trusted adult can make you feel much better.

liked Paula. She had been scared at first, after hearing so many stories from her friends about bad stepmothers and how mean they were. But Paula was different. She did not try to tell Sheryl what to do or act like her mother. She was just very nice and seemed as though she wanted to be Sheryl's friend. One weekend Sheryl's father had to work on Saturday. Sheryl was upset because they had made plans to go to the movies and then out for pizza. However, she still got to go to the movies and have pizza. Paula took her, and they had a great time. Then they met her father later.

When Sheryl came home from her father's house on Sunday evening, her mother asked her how the weekend was and what she did. When Sheryl told her how Paula had taken her out because her dad had had to work, Sheryl's mother frowned. "That's typical of your father," she said. "He can never come through and do what he promised. Always has to have someone else bail him out."

Sheryl got very upset when her mother said that. This was not the first time her mother had made a rude comment about her father that was not true. She really did not want to hear comments like that anymore.

Just as you may be resentful or jealous of your stepparent for the role that he or she is trying to play or the

At first, you may feel disloyal when you spend time with a stepparent.

fact that this person has diverted some of your parent's attention, be aware that your natural parent may actually feel the same way about your other parent's new spouse. The previous scenario is a typical reaction of a mother's jealousy toward her child's stepmother. Sheryl's mother suddenly felt threatened by her daughter's stepmother, who was acting more like a friend than a parent, and was afraid that Sheryl enjoyed spending time with her more than she enjoyed spending time with her mother. As a defense mechanism, Sheryl's mother lashed out at Sheryl's father.

One of the biggest difficulties for a teen whose parents are divorced is the fact that he or she is often constantly being pulled back and forth between the parents. It is very hard for the parents to put the child's needs ahead of their own anger and resentment toward each other. The parents frequently start to bad-mouth each other in front of the child, and they may also criticize a stepparent, especially if it seems as though the child is developing a good relationship with this person.

If you are in this situation, do not be afraid to talk to your parent when he or she makes comments about your other parent that make you upset. Often if parents know how much this behavior is bothering

It is best to talk openly about the things that upset you.

their child, they will realize that they are simply being selfish and are making an already rough situation even worse. As we mentioned earlier, it is important for teens to realize that it is okay to like their stepparent. Sometimes it is just hard for a parent to see his or her child forming a bond with a stepparent, particularly when it is the new spouse of a former spouse. Just as you may need reassurance from your parent that he or she is not being "taken away" by your new step-parent, your natural parent may need reassurance from you that he or she isn't being replaced either.

CHAPTER 5

Making the Family Work

Getting used to your new blended family is no easy task, but bear in mind that it is probably not easy for any of the other family members either. Just as you need time to adjust to your new stepparent and/or stepsiblings, they need time to adjust to you. It takes a lot of effort on everybody's part to make the blended family work.

There are several things a blended family can do to help guide them through the rough spots of creating their family dynamic, and one of these things is to identify what they have in common. Members of blended families have all experienced significant losses. If the family mourn their losses together, it will help them overcome grief and simultaneously form new bonds with one another. As a teenager, if your parents are divorced, you may feel great sadness about it, and you may think that nobody can understand what you are going through. However, if you now have stepsiblings who also went through divorce, try talking to them about your experiences. You may be surprised to find that they are probably feeling the same emotions of grief and anger, and talking about these reactions to one another can help you not to feel so alone. The same goes for teens with a parent who has died: Talking to another teen who knows the pain of losing a parent may help in coping with the loss.

Blended families must also develop new skills and learn how to make decisions as a group. At first it may seem strange, but with the guidance of the parents, the family will begin to form its own identity. As we discussed earlier, change is a major factor in the formation and success of a blended family. Once the members of the family all come to terms with the situation and begin to work together as one unit, instead of two, the blended family can be considered a real family, not a forced unification. Have your parents get everyone together for a family meeting so that each member can openly discuss his or her thoughts and ideas. Your parents and other siblings may be just as anxious as you about where they stand in the family structure, and you may be surprised at how getting together to talk about fears and anxieties can prove to be quite helpful. You must also be open to compromise. Try to accept new ideas and perhaps ways of doing things that differ from the ways you used to do them. Give new ideas a chance before you dismiss them simply because "that's not the way we used to do it." One of the biggest obstacles blended families face is that they have limited shared family histories or shared ways of doing things, and they may have very different beliefs. If you can try to be open to new circumstances and responsibilities within the family, new traditions will arise.

Family Therapy

In many cases, it is easier for blended families to work through their transition with the help of a counselor. In chapter four, we emphasized the benefits of finding someone to talk to and express your feelings to. This may help on a group basis as well, by bringing the entire family to counseling sessions to talk out any problems. Again, an objective listener can be a great asset. Not only will a counselor lend an unbiased ear, but he or she will also provide suggestions and solutions for solving any problems family members are having after listening to what each person has to say. Counselors can act as intermediaries between family members having a dispute. By doing this they will have more of a chance to help the family assess the situation and try to solve the dispute than if the family members continue to battle it out at home. This can be very helpful if there are multiple children, either teens or others, in the family, as they usually have the hardest time in their adjustment. Teens are at such a trying stage of life already that if they suddenly find themselves having to live with another teen, problems can arise. Very often two people fighting, especially teens, become stubborn and selfish and cannot see the other person's side unless it is shown to them through the skills of an intermediary.

It is also beneficial to continue going as a group to the counseling sessions over a long period of time. This way the counselor becomes the family's friend and advisor and has the chance to watch the family dynamic develop and improve with time. After a while, the counselor will be able to assess the progress that has been made and advise the family members on how to continue working together and solving their problems.

Your family may need
therapy to cope.

Looking at Your Parents' Needs

As a teenager, it certainly will not be an easy transition to the blended family. However, there are several things to consider aside from the fact that the blended family may not be exactly what you had in mind for your life. Teens often forget that the life changes that affect them affect their parents as well. If you have experienced the divorce of your parents, it was undoubtedly hard on you. Try taking a minute to think about your parents' feelings, too. Even if they were in an unhappy relationship and it was in their best interest to get divorced, the breakup of a marriage is still extremely painful. Suddenly they are single, and this time as parents. That is no easy task.

Although as a teenager you are dealing with seemingly endless problems, take a moment to think like an adult and put yourself in your parents' shoes. Try to realize that they are dealing with major changes as well. It may help to look at them as people and not just as your parents. The popular phrase "Parents are people too" says it best. Just as you need someone to talk to about your anxieties, so do they. In particular, try to think about this when parents begin dating again and perhaps meet someone they like. Don't they deserve to be happy, too? Very often a divorced person finds solace in talking to another divorced person and hearing how he or she handled problems. Just as you can relate to your peers and friends, your parents can relate to theirs. For a parent to find another parent who has been through a divorce or who understands what it is like to lose a spouse can be extremely comforting. It is just as we discussed in chapter four regarding how support groups are helpful for both you and your parents.

Even while trying to adjust to the blended family, there will always be a need for you to spend time alone with your natural parent. The bond between you and your parent is still very important. Having special time alone with your parent will help you in your adjustment to the blended family. It will provide an outlet for you to speak privately with your parent and express any feelings and anxieties you may be having. In addition, this time together can be an assurance that you have not lost your parent during the formation of the blended family. Not only do teenagers often resent their stepparent for being the new person their parent relies on, as we mentioned earlier, but they may also fear that their parent is going to be "taken away" from them by their stepparent. Spending time alone together will allow you and your parent to have a little time out just to enjoy being together, and it will reassure you that your parent is not being "taken away."

The Positives

Blended families are full of positive elements, although you may not see them right away. It is important to note that having a stepparent does not mean that anyone expects you to forget about your mom or dad who has died or, in the case of divorce, does not live with you anymore. Being in a blended family simply means that you have more people in your life. There may be more siblings who are close to your age and can ultimately turn into new friends. There may also be more grandparents, aunts, uncles, and cousins. The addition of these people to your life can add not only to the number of people in your family but to the warmth and happiness within the family as well. Remember, you have not lost the people in your old family—you have just gained an extended family.

Blended families
have a lot of
positive aspects.

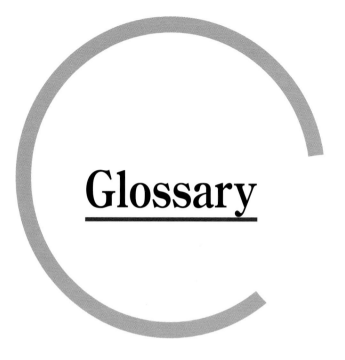

Glossary

adolescence   The time of development between puberty and adulthood; the teenage years.

blended family   A family that forms when two adults get married and at least one of them has a child or children from a previous marriage; also known as a stepfamily.

divorce   The termination of a marriage.

half sibling   The child of your natural parent and stepparent.

natural family   The family that exists before divorce and remarriage, usually made up of parents and their biological children.

natural parent   A parent who is biologically related to you.

stepparent   The person your parent marries, either after your natural parents have divorced or one parent has died.

stepsibling   The child of the person your parent marries.

Where to Go for Help

In the United States

Childhelp

(800) 422-4453
Hotline for young people in crisis.

Children's Rights Council

300 I Street NE
Suite 401
Washington, DC 20002
(202) 547-6227
Web site: http://www.vix.com/crc/

Stepfamily Association of America

650 J Street

Suite 205

Lincoln, NE 68508

(402) 477-7837

(800) 735-0329

Web site: http://www.stepfam.org

The Stepfamily Foundation, Inc.

333 West End Avenue

New York, NY 10023

(212) 877-3244

Fax: (212) 362-7030

Twenty-four-hour information line: (212) 799-STEP

Web site: http://www.stepfamily.org

The Stepfamily Network

2600 Central Avenue

Suite L

Union City, CA 84587

(800) 487-1073

Web site: www.stepfamily.net

In Canada

Canadian Youth Rights Association
27 Bainbridge Avenue
Nepean, ON K2G 3T1
(613) 721-1004
Web site: http://www.cyra.org

Family Service Canada
404-383 Parkdale Avenue
Ottawa, ON K1Y 4R4
(613) 722-9006
Web site: http://www.cfc-efc.ca/fsc/

Web Sites

My Two Homes
http://www.mytwohomes.com/
A site where young people can order cool stuff to
make life with two homes easier: a calendar to
keep track of days with each parent, a handbook,
a photo album, and more.

The Kids Corner
http://www.eros.thepark.com/volunteer/safehaven/
divorce/divorce_kids.htm

For young people whose families are going through
or have been through a divorce, with links to sites
specifically for teens and sites in Canada as well.

The Kids' Page at Successful Steps
http://www.positivesteps.com/Kids.htm
Lots of information amd support for kids about stepfamilies, parents, siblings, abandonment, and
other subjects.

For Further Reading

American Bar Association Family Law Section. *My Parents Are Getting Divorced: A Handbook for Kids*. Chicago: American Bar Association, 1996.

Bolick, Nancy O. *How to Survive Your Parents' Divorce*. Danbury, CT: Franklin Watts, 1995.

Fenwick, Elizabeth, and Tony Smith. *Adolescence: The Survival Guide for Parents and Teenagers*. New York: Dorling Kindersley, 1993.

Johnson, Linda Carlson. *Everything You Need to Know About Your Parents' Divorce*. Rev. ed. New York: Rosen Publishing Group, 1998.

Joselow, Beth, and Thea Joselow. *When Divorce Hits Home: Keeping It Together When Your Family Comes Apart.* New York: Avon Books, 1996.

Park, Barbara. *My Mother Got Married and Other Disasters.* New York: Alfred A. Knopf, 1990.

Scheider, Meg F., Joan Zuckerberg, and Joan Offernman-Zuckerberg. *Difficult Questions Kids Ask and Are Afraid to Ask About Divorce.* New York: Fireside, 1996.

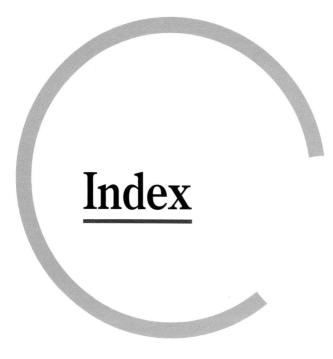

Index

T
talking, 7, 13, 14, 37, 39, 42, 46,
        47, 50
tension, 11, 36

W
withdrawal, 31

About the Author

Julie Leibowitz is a freelance editor based in New York.
This is her first Rosen book.

Photo Credits

Cover and pp. 4, 12, 16, 27, 30, 34, 38, 41, 43, 49, 53
by Thaddeus Harden;   pp.18, 20 © The Everett
Collection; p. 25 © Index Stock.

Design and Layout

Michael Caroleo

Series Editor

Erica Smith